Doris Marjorie Moore's

50

COMMON

HOUSEHOLD

ITEMS

THAT

REPEL

OR

ABSORB

ELECTROMAGNETIC

RADIATION

VOLUME 1

Electromagnetic field is created around every electric conductor when an electric current is running through it...
In electric appliances there are wires, electronic components, etc... When turned on these components and wires emit electromagnetic radiation in the frequencies of the electric network...

The way to reduce electromagnetic radiation is to unplug what you are not using....

THE LIST
(current as of 3/11/2016)

1. <u>**ADHESIVES**</u> - actions- Repel/Absorb (present & working on all products listed below)
a. **SHIPPING LABELS**
b. **BARCODE LABELS**
c. **MASKING TAPE**
d. **CLEAR PACKING TAPE**
e. **CARDBOARD BOXES**

2. <u>**BATTERIES**</u> - actions - Absorb... (used or new, even dead ones work)
a. **AAA** b. **AA** c. **C** d. **D**

If you suspect EM around you, take any one of these, hold it on it's sides, not the terminals...Place it close to your body and you will feel the EM move...

3. <u>BUBBLE GUM -</u>

actions- Absorb

a. Not today's bubble gum but the brands that were popular in the 50's,60's & 70's... The chicle is more dense and you can still find those brands on the market today...Pop a piece in your mouth while on a cell phone and you're covered...(no kidding) Unchewed, it still absorbs, but eventually the EM will break it down into a sticky, gooey mess ...

4. CELLOPHANE - action- Repels, Slows Flow...

   a. cigarette pack outer covers (contains static electricity)

   b. candy wrappers (with a twist on either end)

   c. cake wrappers

5. <u>FILTERS</u> - action- Absorbs / Filters

   a. Smoking pipe filters

   b. Cigarette filters

   c. wet sponges

   d. Any fibrous material (pillow stuffing, mattress stuffing,etc.)

5. FILTERS - (continued)

e. Polyester - clothing, throws, etc...

6. METALS - actions - repels, deflects

a. catfood cans with inner lining + lid

b. tabs from any pop top can(top showing deflects, bottom showing repels)

c. Cutlery - esp. spoon and fork (curve repels)

d. Aluminum Foil - I found this one on the internet, when I first realized what I was dealing with...

6. <u>METALS</u> - (continued)

d. aluminum foil...
I was told to wallpaper my walls with it... And so I did, however I learned much later that it doesn't come through the walls, but through the windows. And so I finally covered the windows with it and got some relief... In Fact, there is very little on the net about it and yet we are surrounded by it everyday...

7. <u>MAKE-UP AND MOISTERIZERS</u> -

action - repels

a. eye shadow
b. foundation make-up
c. lipstick & lipgloss
d. skin lotions of almost any type
e. nail polish
f. spf protection from the sun.

8. PAPER - action - absorbs

I have come to the conclusion that it is the adhesives used to bind the wood pulp into paper that makes it work...

8. PAPER - (continued)

Almost any type will work, especially if rolled into a tube...The best of the bunch is listed below...

a. Packing or shipping

b. Newspaper (with print works best)

c. Wrapping Paper

d. Printer Paper

A special note here concerning cardboard boxes... If you take any size empty cardboard box, seal it closed with one of the tapes mentioned earlier...Then poke a hole in every side of the box including top and bottom, you have essentially created an electromagnetic filter...I've done it many times and it works...

9. __PLASTICS__ - action - Repels/Absorbs

This is a very broad category, but let's stick with the most recent you purchase...

a. Soda bottles (2 liter) washed out and filled with water,the cap off. Absorb like crazy!

b. Any white or black tray used to heat food in a microwave (TV dinner type) Repels like a Shield. (The cover you peel back can also be used, inner side up

9. <u>PLASTICS</u>-(continued)
absorbs, inner side
down repels...
  c. Any clear tray from
  baked goods or other
  food stuffs... Repels
  like a Shield...
  d. Small container's
  with a wide mouth,
  used to sell over the
  counter medication...
  upright with a small
  amount of water,
  absorb... Upside down
  with the lid off, Repel..
  e. When the lip balm
  is at the end, leave
  the lid off and stand it
  upside down, absorbs.

10. **<u>POLISH (furniture)</u>** -
    action - Repels
    a. With the first spray applied to wood EM is almost undetectable...
    b. And your furniture looks great, too...

11. **<u>POLYURETHANE</u>** -
    action - Repels
    a. From the moment the can is opened, EM seems to disappear...
    b. My "A" frame home is built with cedar board. It took 7gals to do the interior...

12. <u>POTATO CHIPS</u> - action - absorbs Practically anything organic has an effect of some kind on Electromagnetic Radiation...Broad categories include...

a. All fried food...

b. All gravy's...

c. All charcoal cooked food...

But, the Potato Chip is the most powerful... I've never been sure exactly why... Just one chip set out on a flat surface,seem to shut it down...

13. <u>SILVER</u> - action - Repels
   a. On the internet I found a shirt made from silver thread. It was very expensive... However, I did find other things that worked just as well and didn't cost as much...
   b. Silver necklace
   c. Silver rings
   d. Silver earrings
14. <u>SWIMMING POOL</u> - action - Repels
   a. Keep it clean and it works...

15. **WATER** - action - Repels

    a. You can stand next to a small body of water and not be protected if the water is dirty, so keep it clean...

    b. In any kind of container, except metal. Open or closed lid.

    c. Sprayed on any surface, including yourself...

    d. Drink plenty, EM/ Microwave emissions are very dehydrating...

1. <u>ADVERSE REACTIONS TO ELECTROMAGNETIC/ MICROWAVE RADIATION</u>

a. Fluctuations in blood pressure and heart rate

b. Headache

c. Sleeplessness

d. Ringing in the ears

e. Nausea

f. Memory and Concentration problems

g. Depression

h. Increased risk of cancer.

i. Leukemia

HOW TO AVOID EXPOSURE TO ELECTROMAGNETIC RADIATION

1. Use a secondary mouse and keyboard on your laptop and don't put it in your Lap...

2. Use an LCD monitor, they emit less radiation.

3. Neaten up electrical cords and transformers around your desk and move them away from your immediate area...

4. Avoid Wireless Networks, they emit radiation even when not in use...

5. When shopping for a cordless phone, avoid those that use DECT technology. They emit a very strong signal...

6. Limit your cell phone use, children younger than 14 should be very limited...

7. Unplug all electrical power cords and devices when not in use in the bedroom, to enhance sleep...

8. Avoid using halogen, florescent and compact florescent lighting they can create "dirty electricity" high frequency radiation that emanates from your home's wiring...

9. Replace all the dimmer switches you have with reg on/off...Even when turned on to full power the dimmer chops off part of the electrical current, then discards it in the form of a strong EM field...

10. INSTALL ELECTROMAGNETIC FILTERS...

reference - Kevin Byrne April 24 2009

SOURCES EMITTING EMF/EMR

1. REFRIGERATORS

2. AIR FANS

3. BABY MONITORS

4. DESKTOP COMPUTERS

5. LAPTOP COMPUTERS

6. ELECTRIC STOVES

7. AIR CONDITIONERS

8. ELECTRIC BEDS

9. FISH TANK FILTERS

SOURCES EMITTING EMF/EMR

10. IPHONE

11. SMART PHONES

12. CELL PHONES

13. BLUETOOTH

14. BLACKBERRY

15. WI-FI

16. IPOD TOUCH

17. PS3

18. WII

SOURCES EMITTING EMF/EMR

19. XBOX 360

20. WI-FI ROUTER

21. POWER TOOLS

22. PRINTERS

23. TV'S AND MONITORS

24. MICROWAVE OVENS

25. WASHER/DRYER

JUST TO NAME A FEW... THANKS
DMMOORE